Tales Of Wonder

Adel Lee

ISBN:1543050050
ISBN-13:9781543050059

"Tales Of Wonder" is a colouring book intended for people of all ages. The wonderful fairy-tale themed designs, are both simple and complex, with different styles of art to diversify each and every page.

All the funds received from this book will go to charity

I hope that you enjoy it!

Adel Lee

ACKNOWLEDGMENTS

A huge thanks to Jana al Faras for contributing her pieces to the book and, Jolana, for giving me advice and encouragement about the project constantly.

Finally, as always, my parents for supporting me through thick and thin with their experiences and suggestions on how to improve the book.

Adel's Tall Tales

Little Red Riding Hood,

look how wonderful the flowers are!

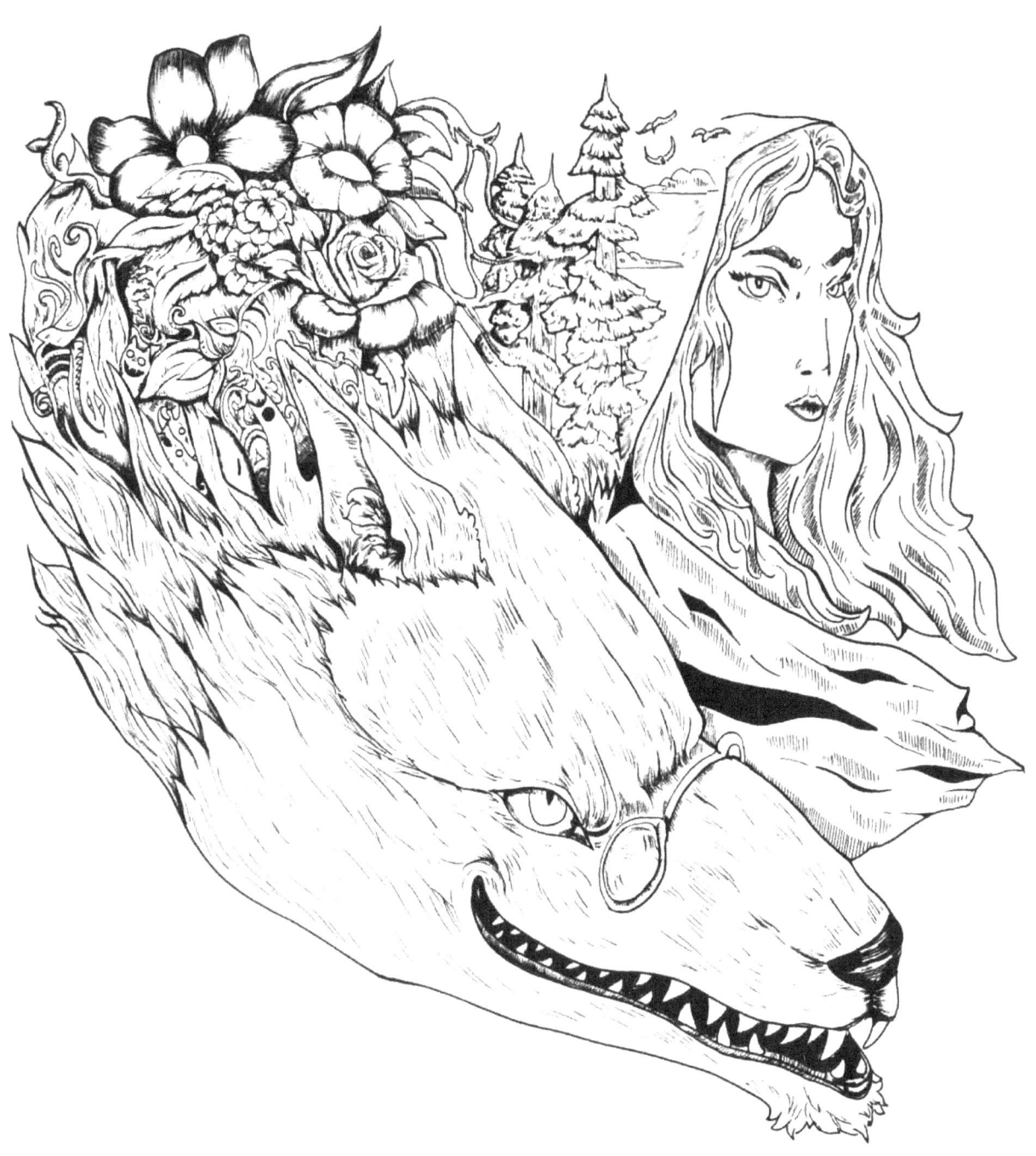

As she devoured the coin, her body became luminous

and she could see the cave walls littered with precious stone

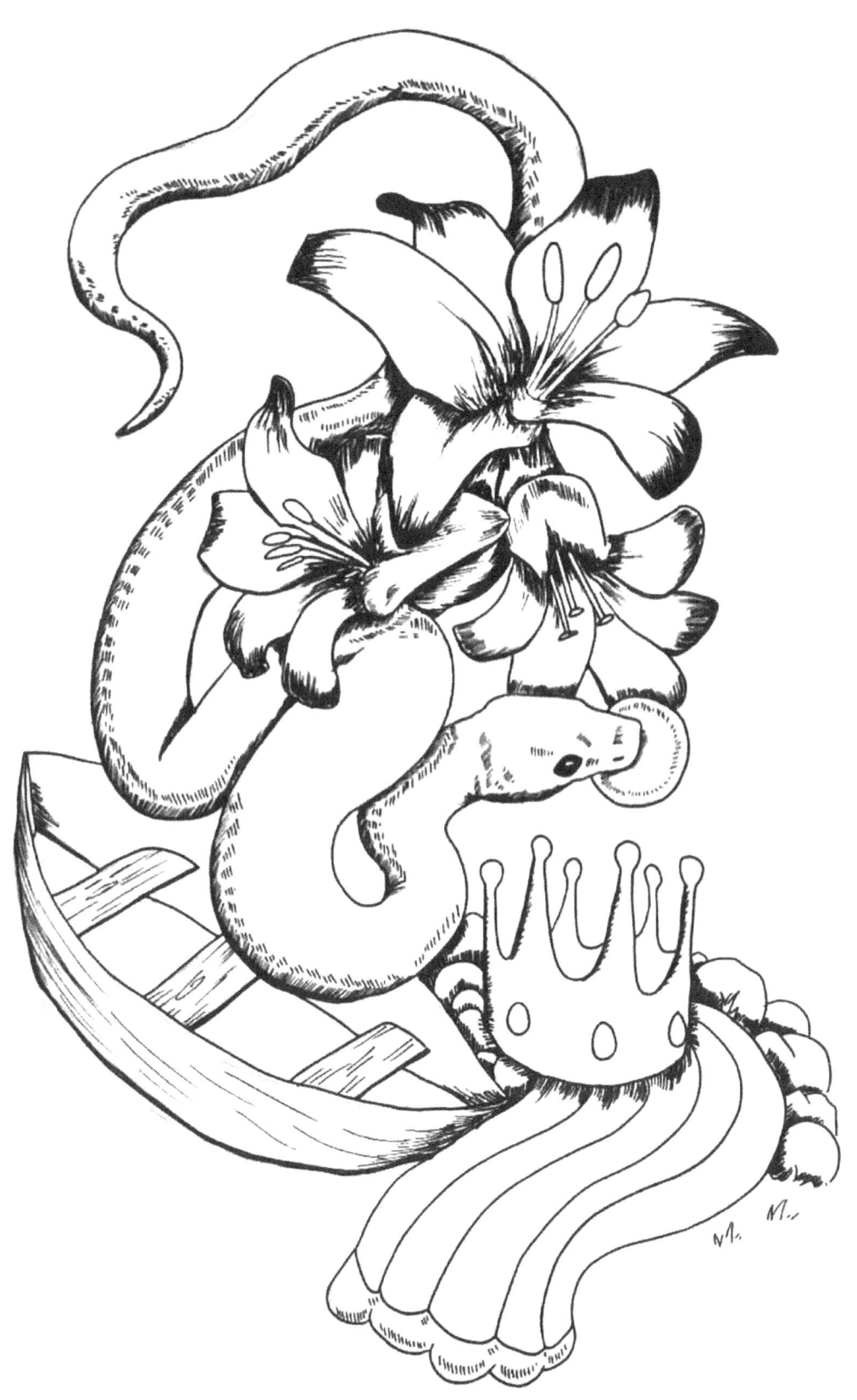

Redemption includes remorse but you lie here guiltless and despondent.

Oh what shall we do with you?

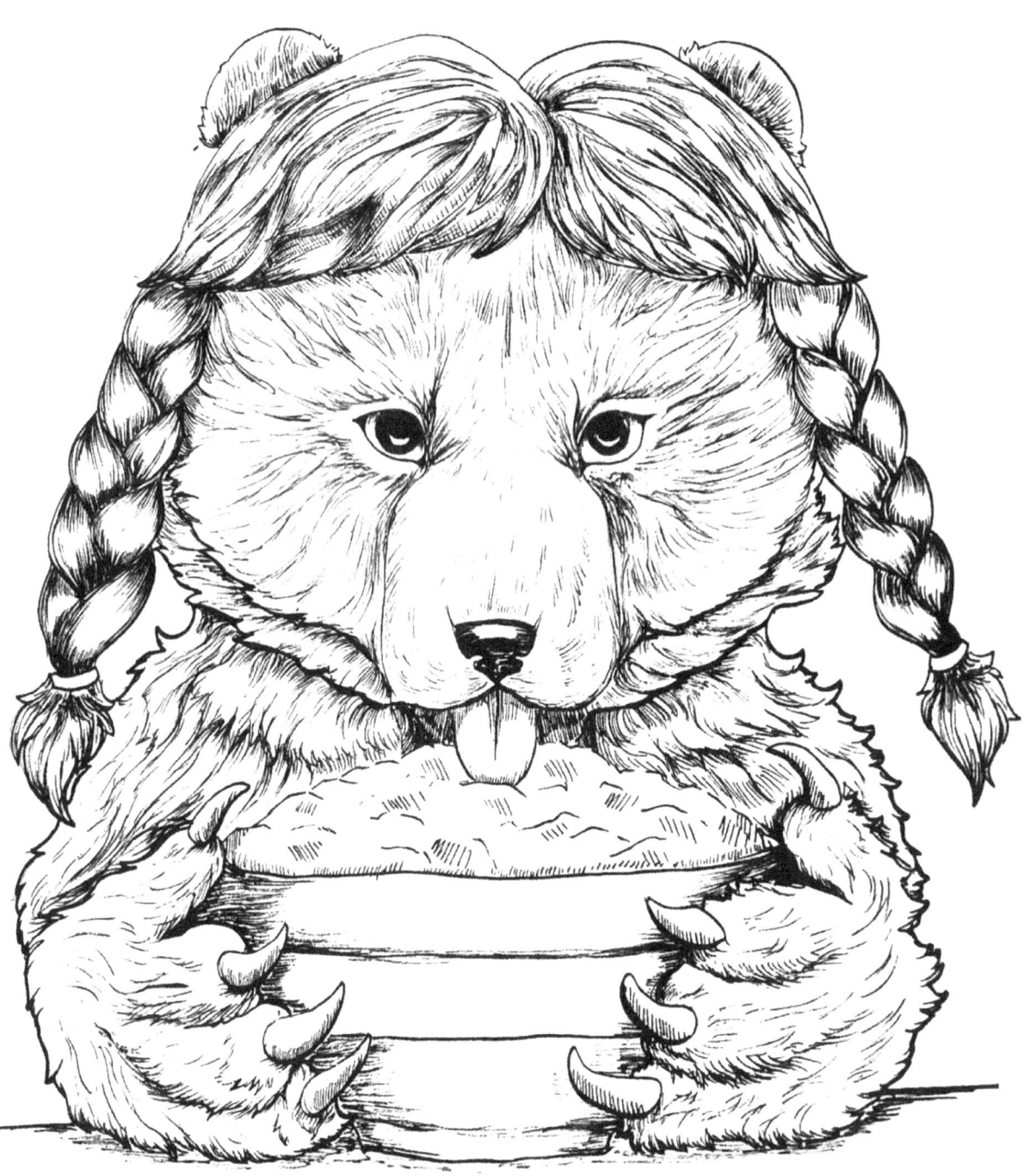

What is my Life in comparison to Love?

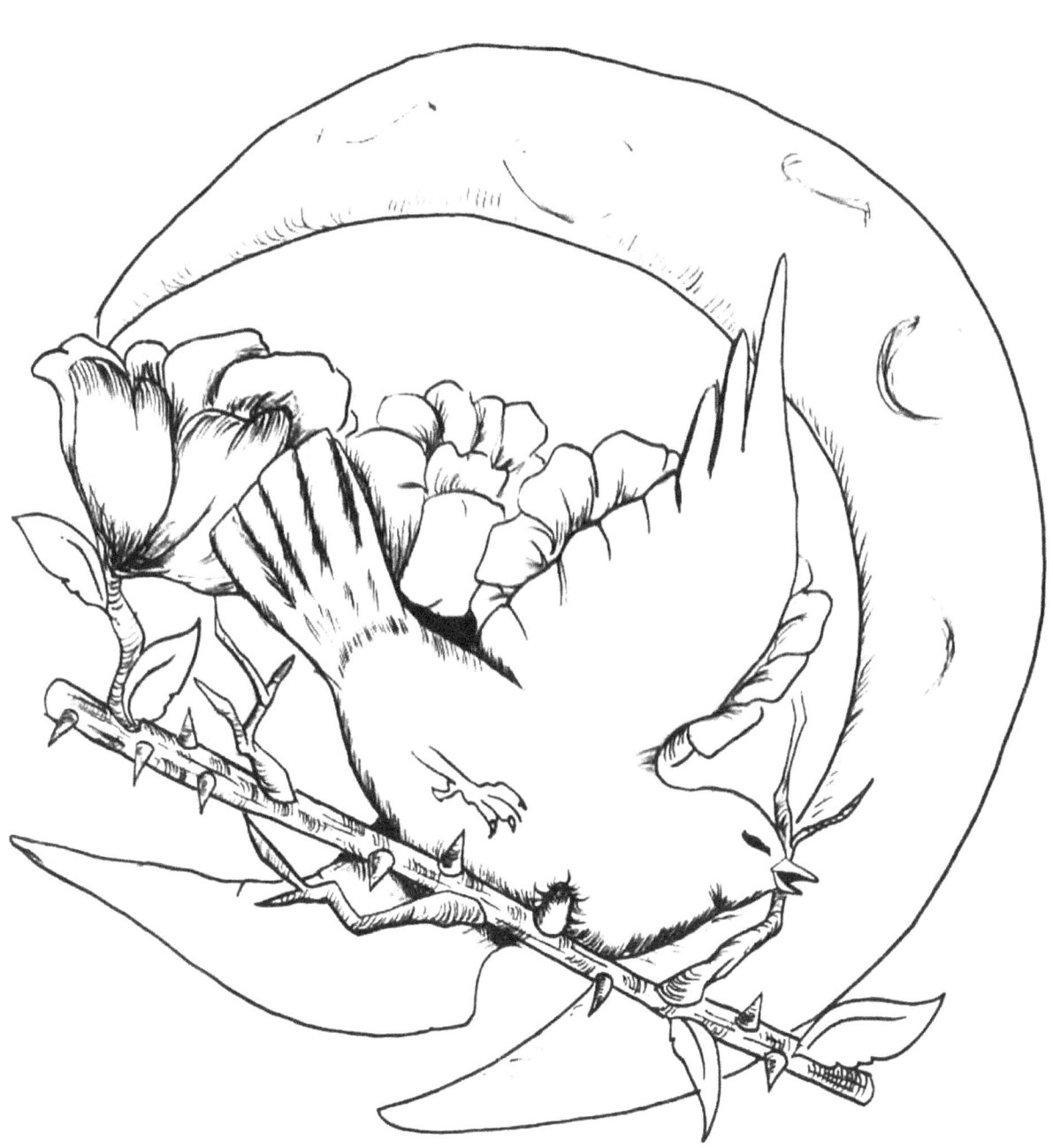

The mouse was terrified.

He trembled at the sight of the lion.

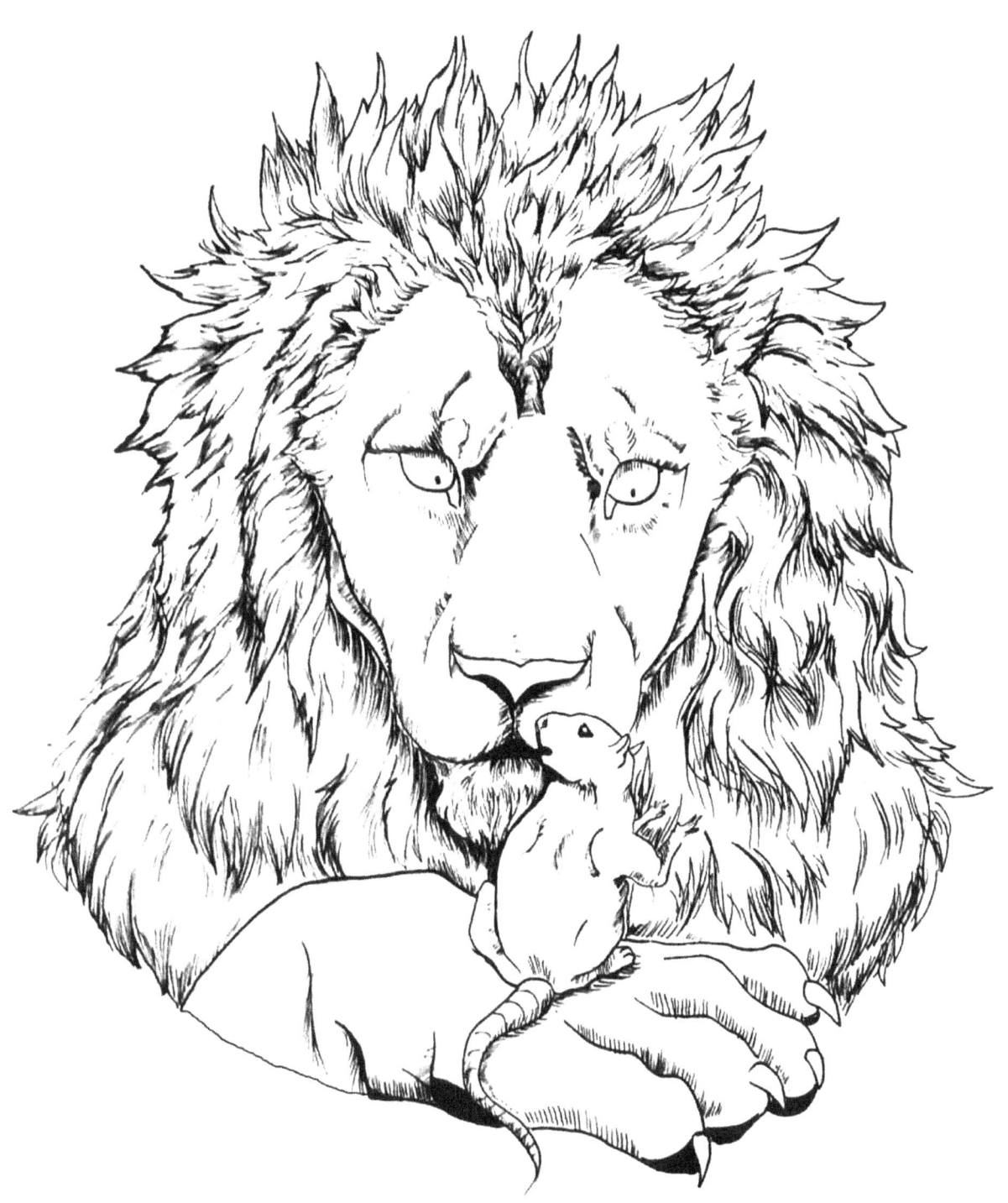

Within the crown of antlers,

a young girl sleeps peacefully

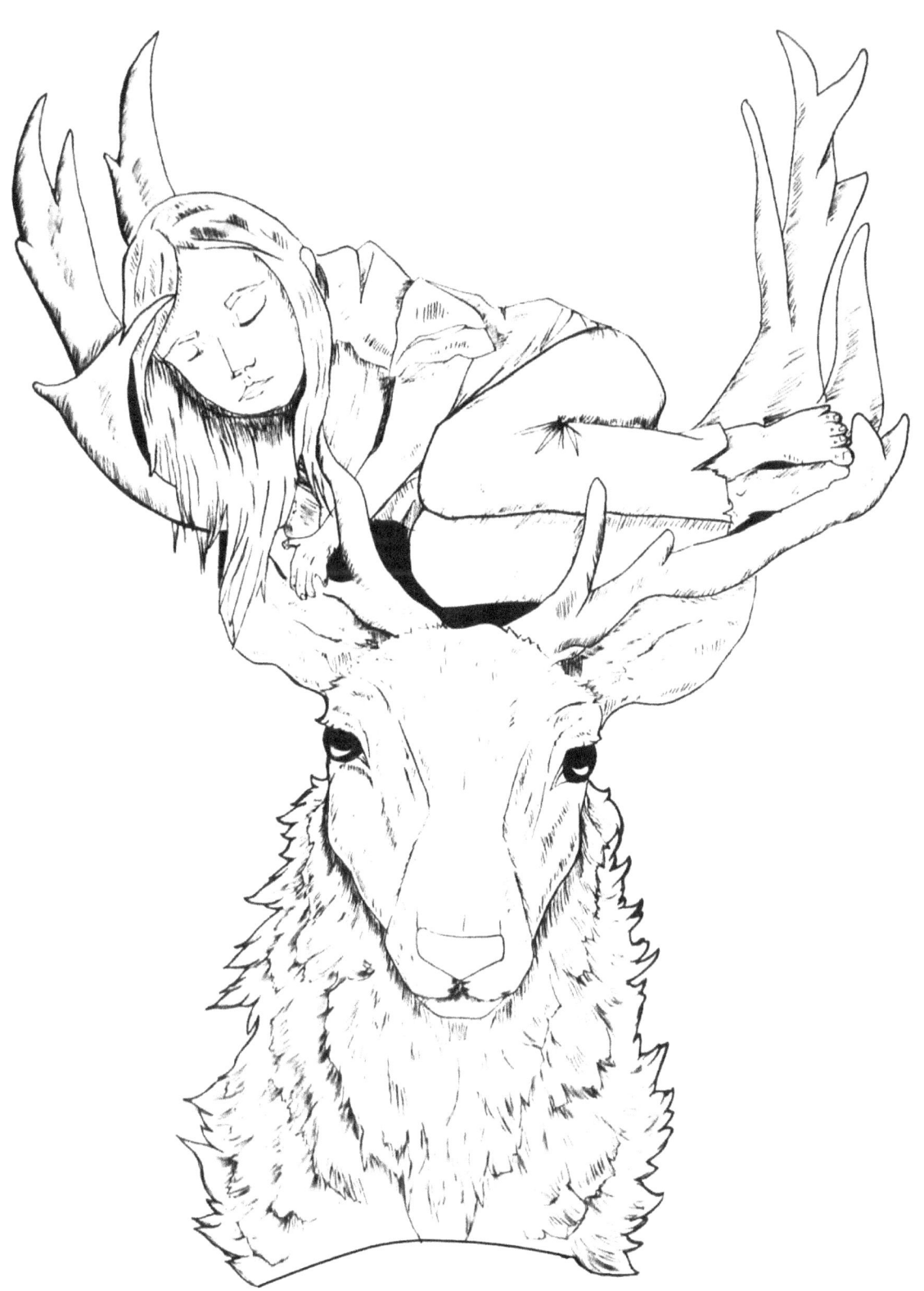

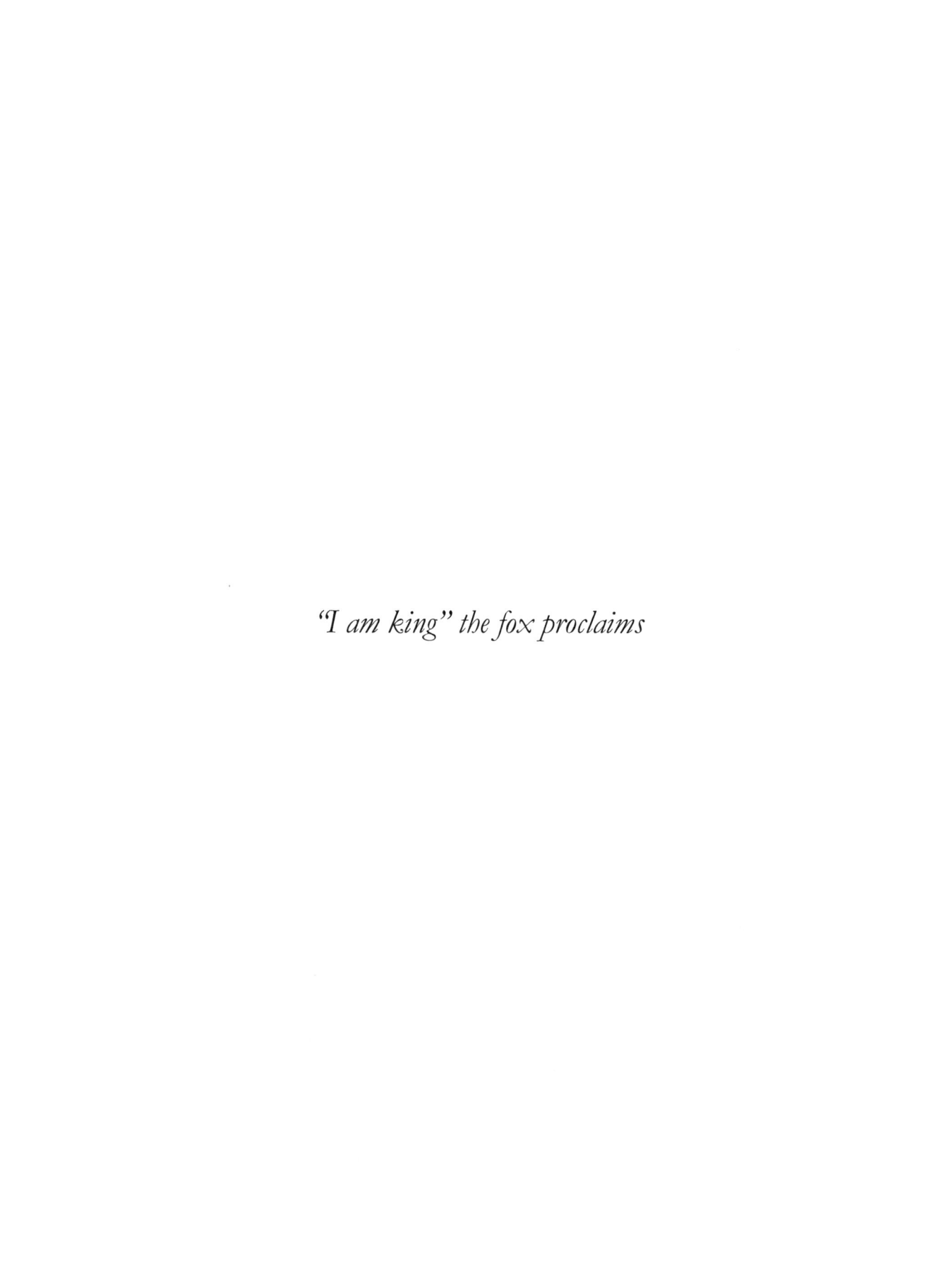

"I am king" the fox proclaims

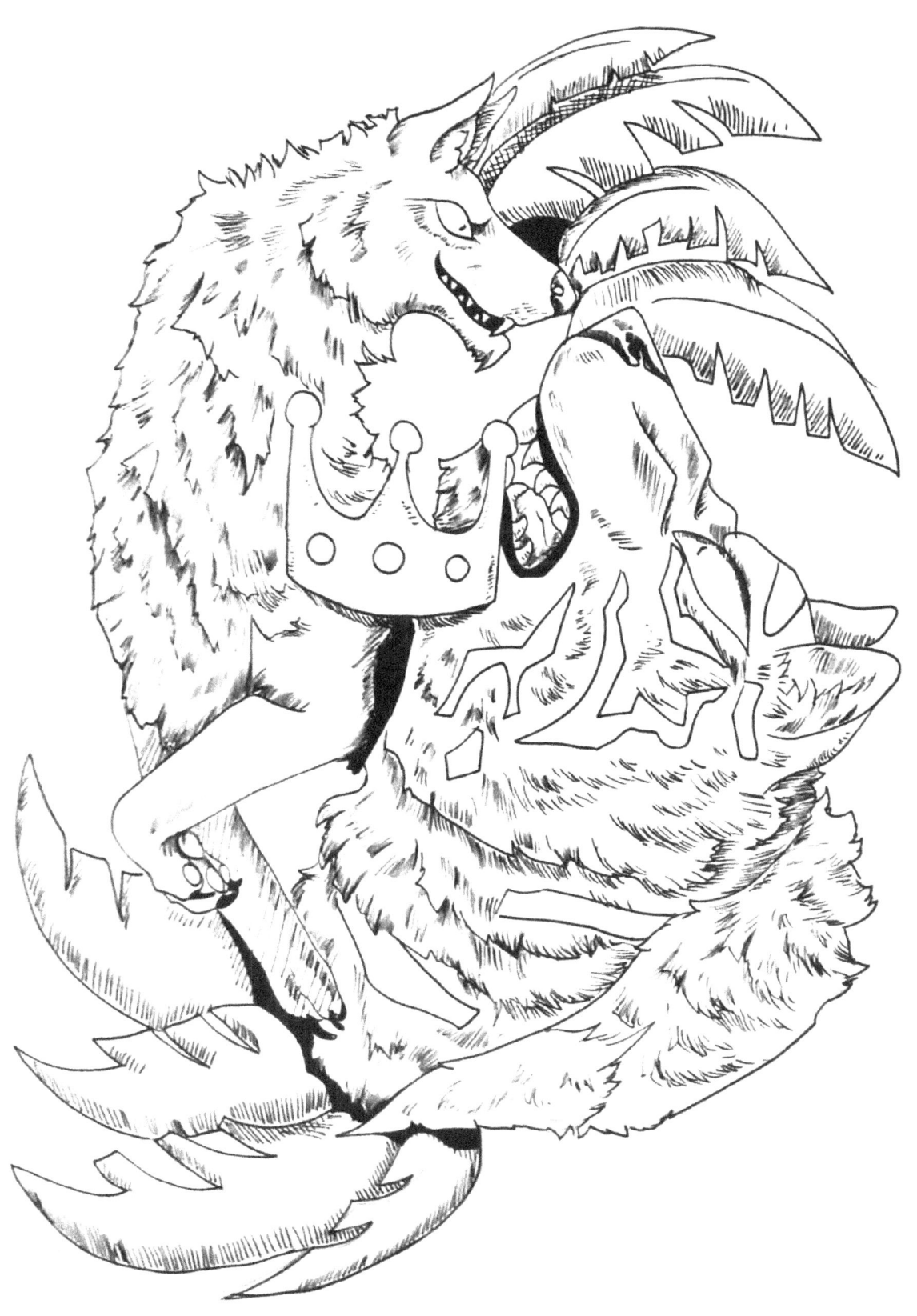

Griffin Cubs are the hardest to train

as their mischievous natures tempts them to rebel.

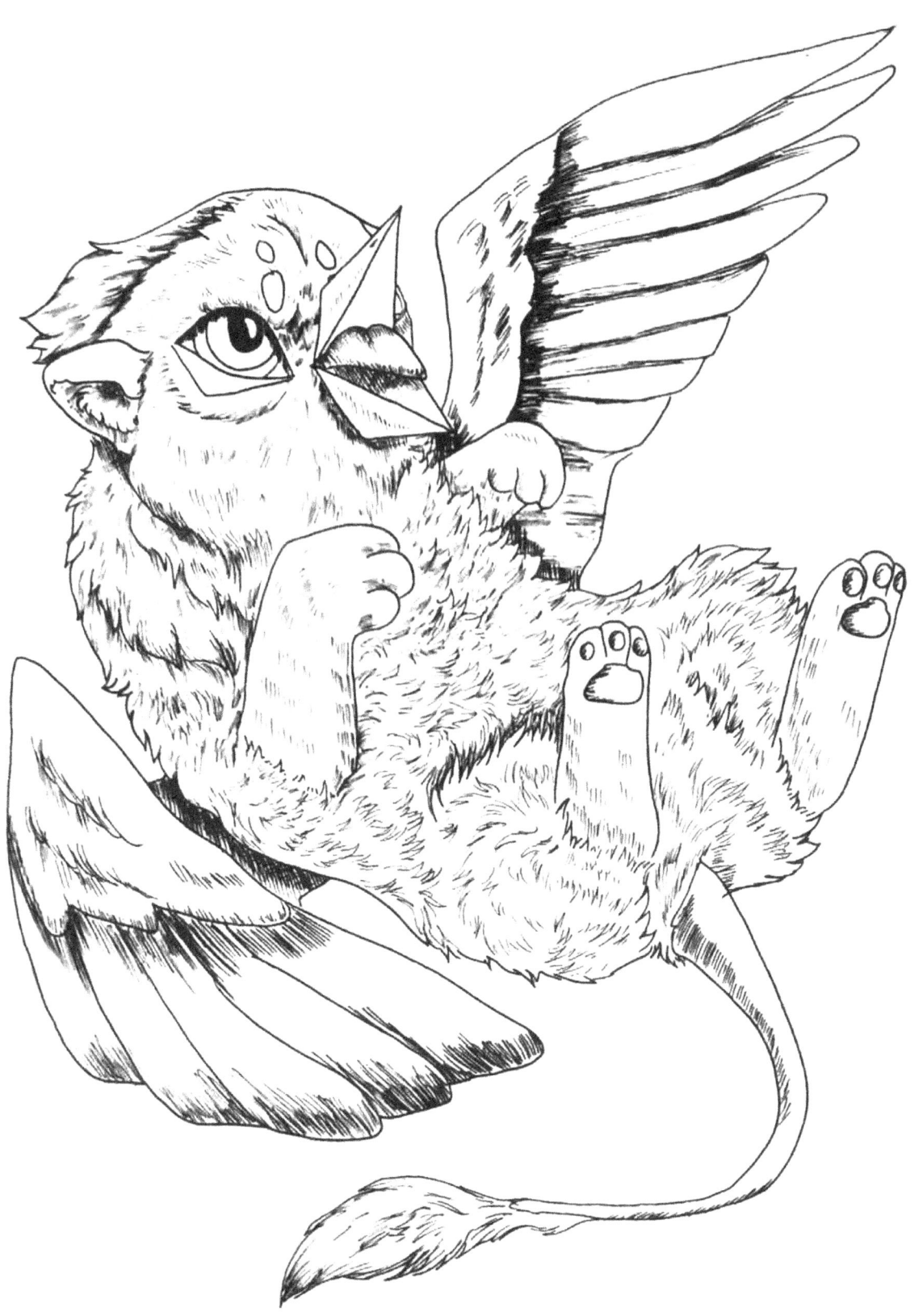

Its wisdom spans centuries of human thinking.

The dragon rests under the mountains.

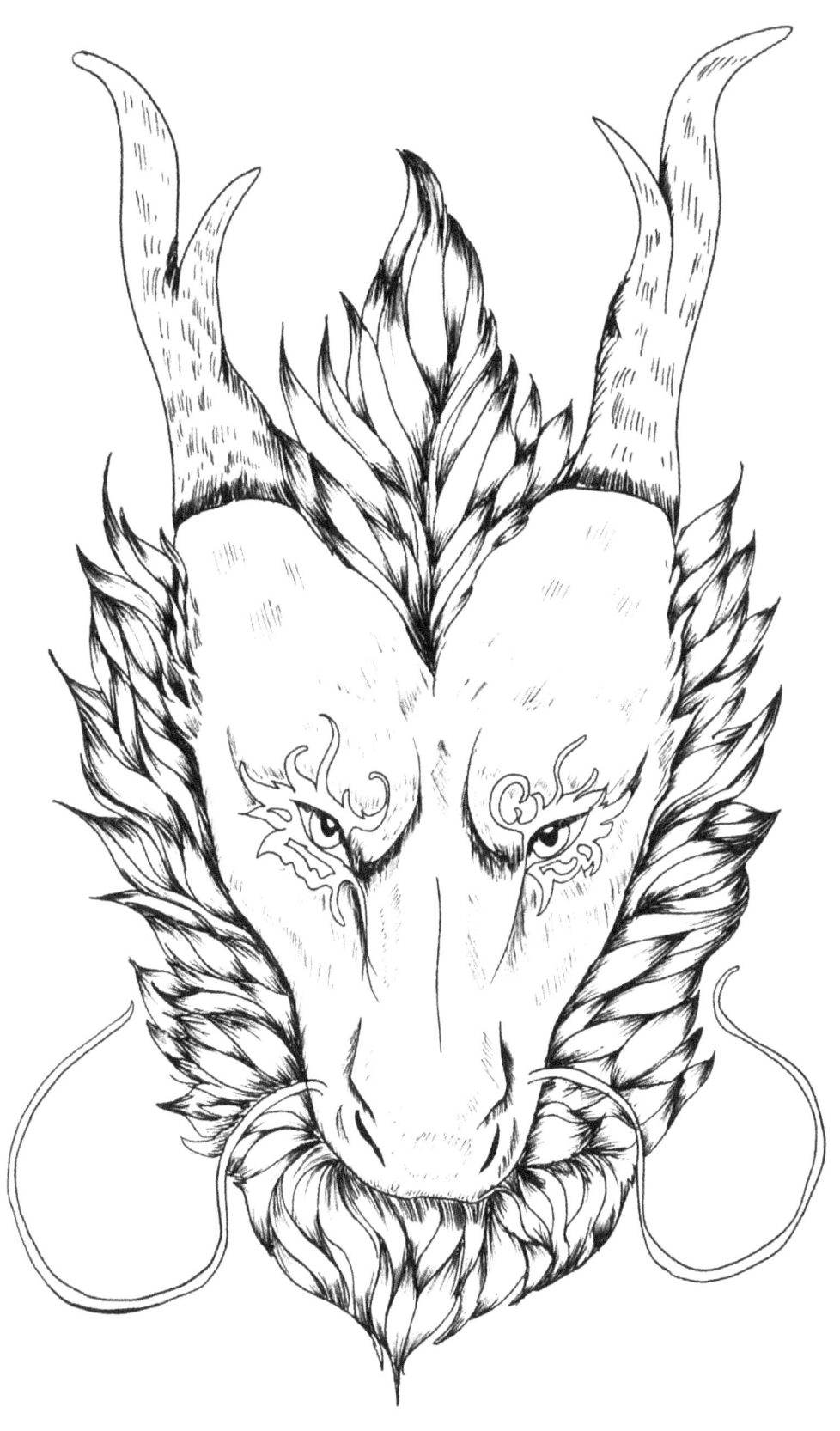

Banging on the doors of the dungeon,

poor Belle's cries fell on deaf ears.

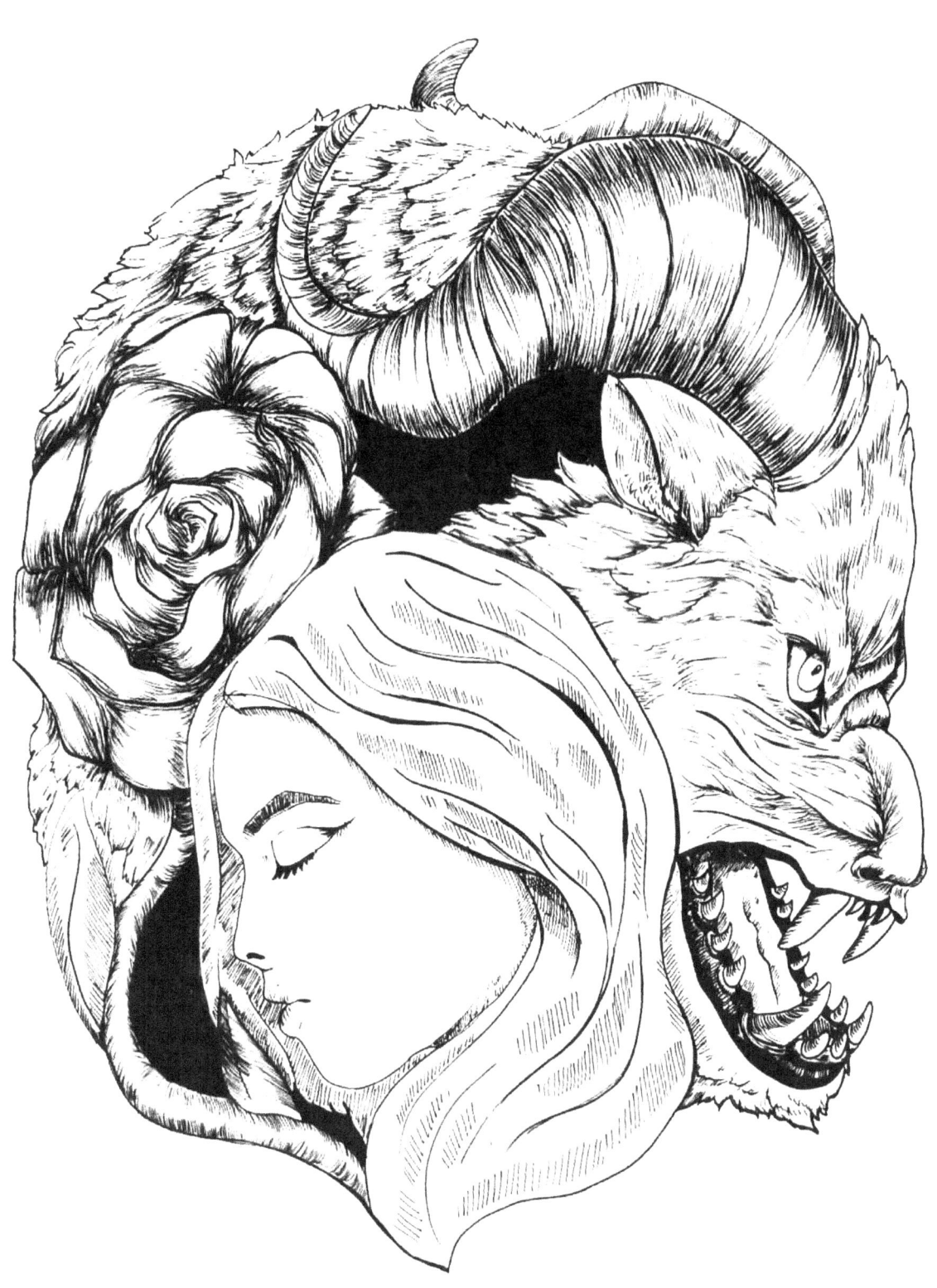

A dance under the moonlight, a sonata with the stars,

I would do everything for you.

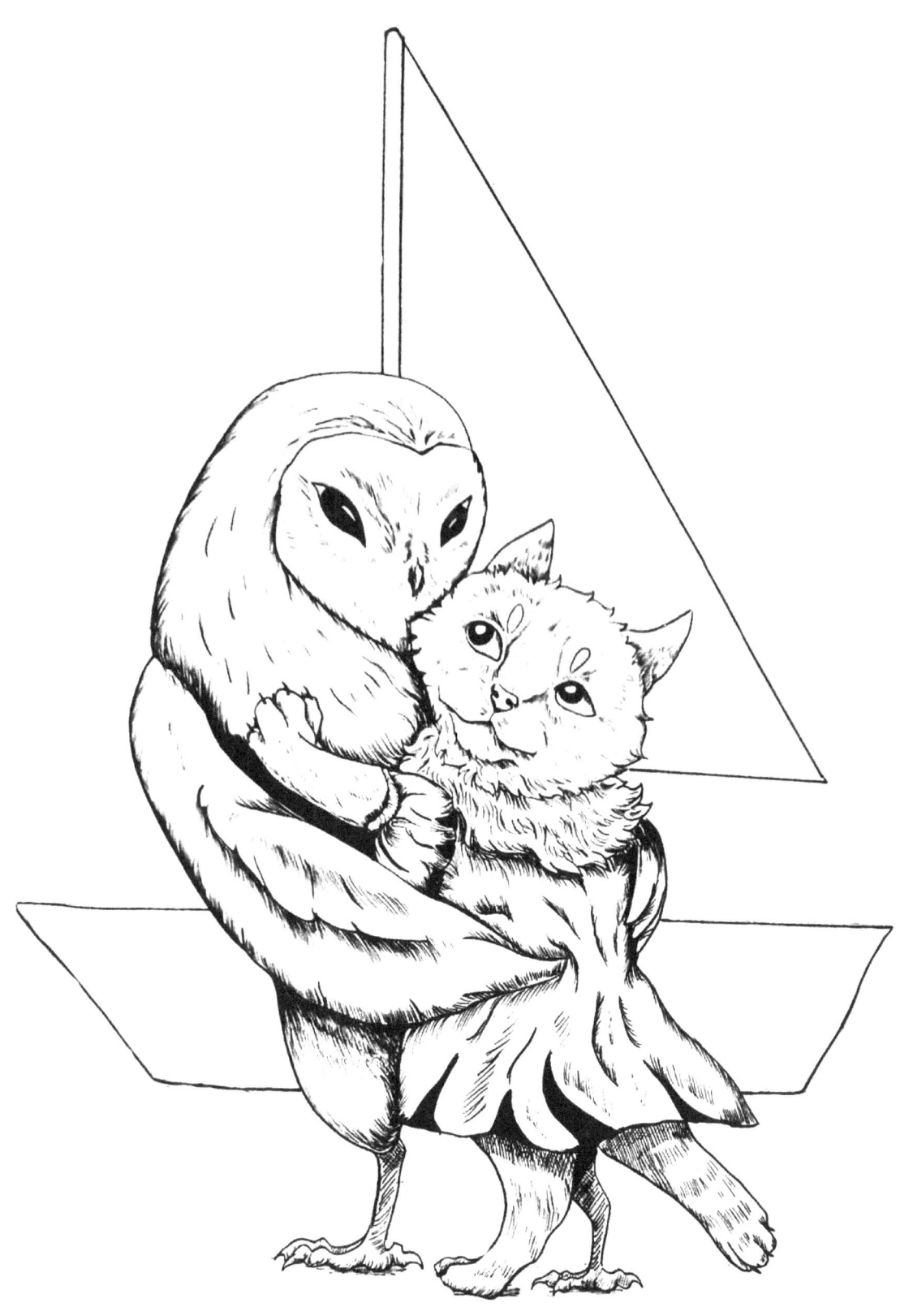

In his reflection was the most handsome swan

he had ever seen.

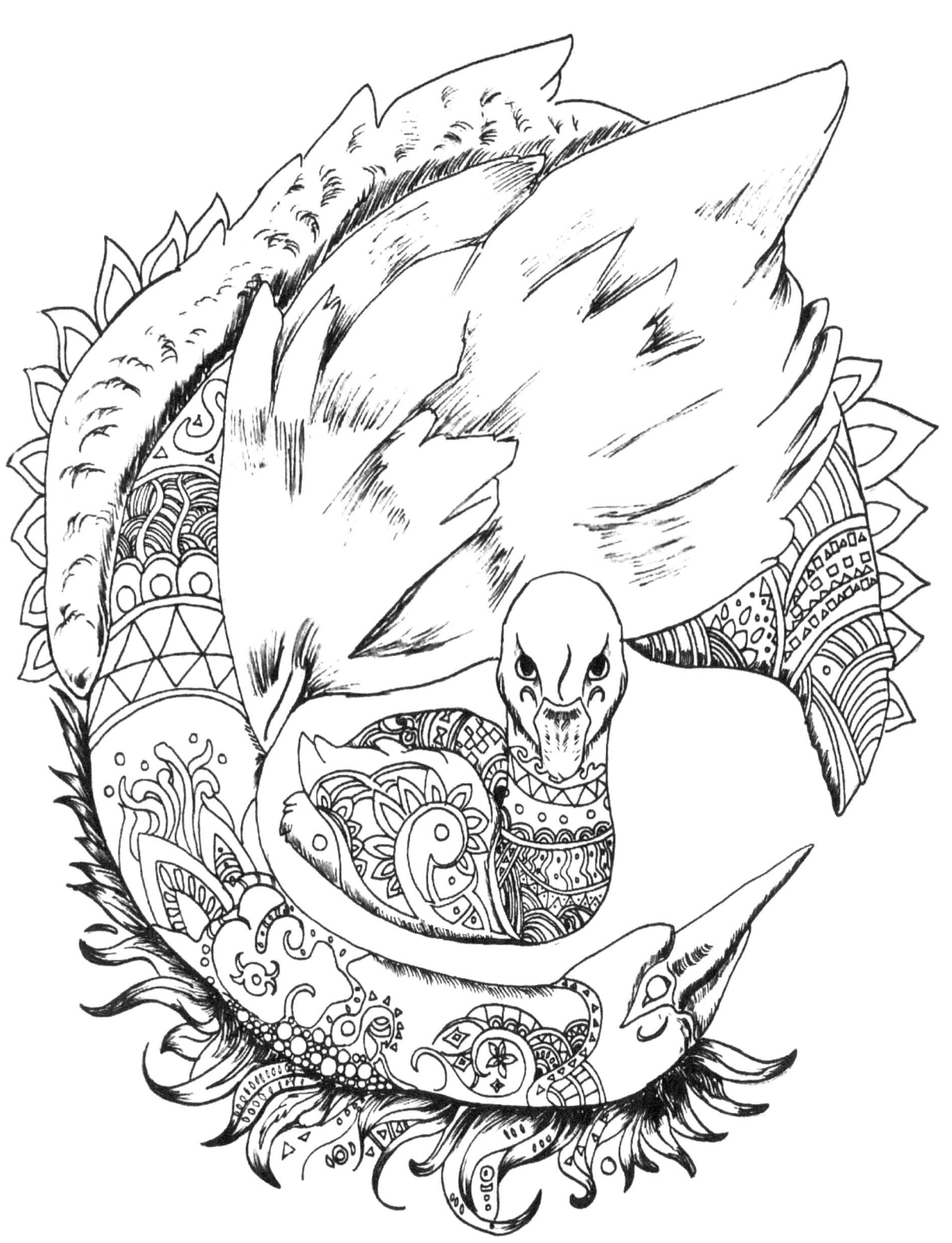

In the case of the tortoise and the hare,

hard work prevailed over laziness.

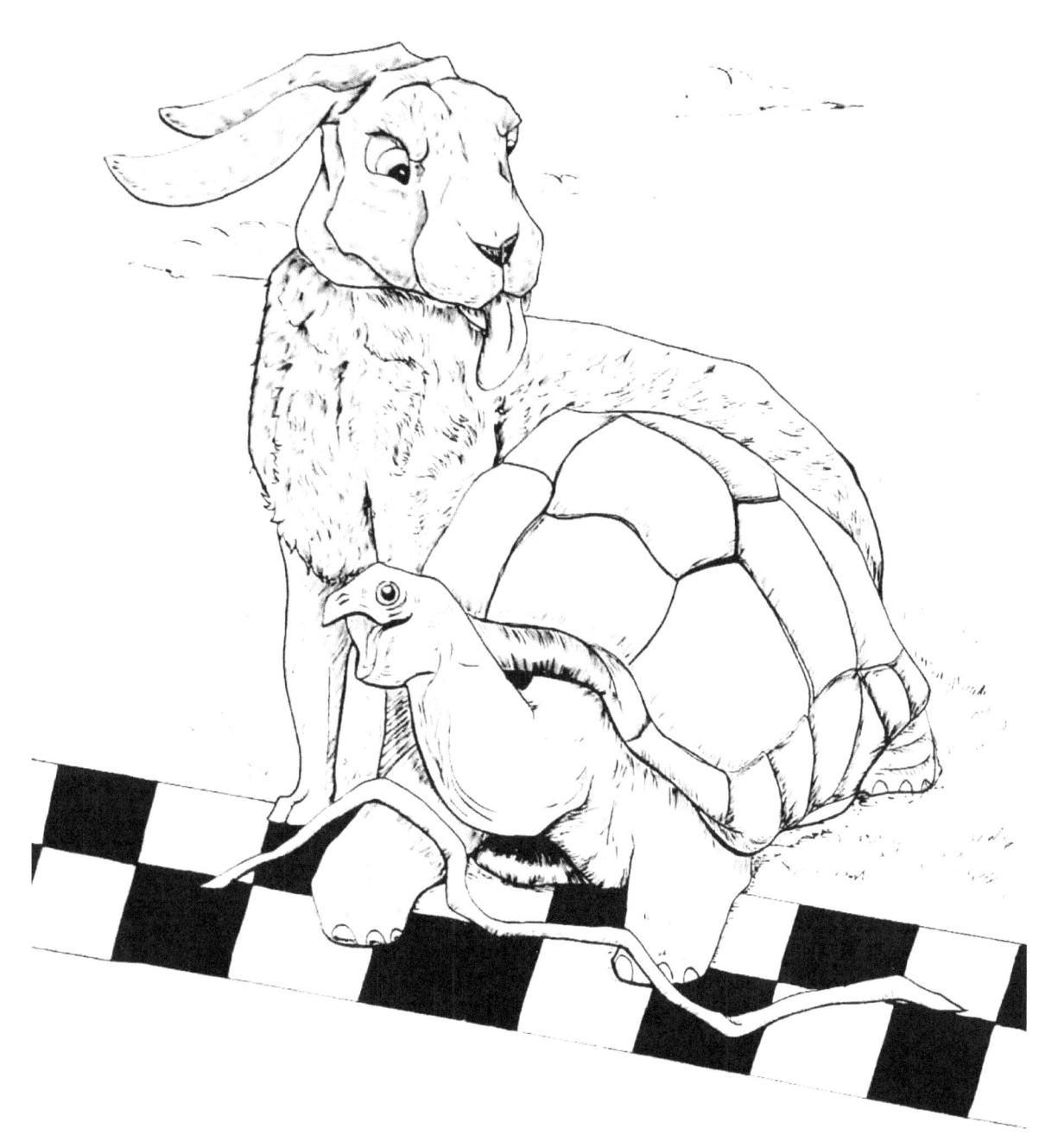

Its words pounded on their skulls.

Vicious Lies masquerading as Truth.

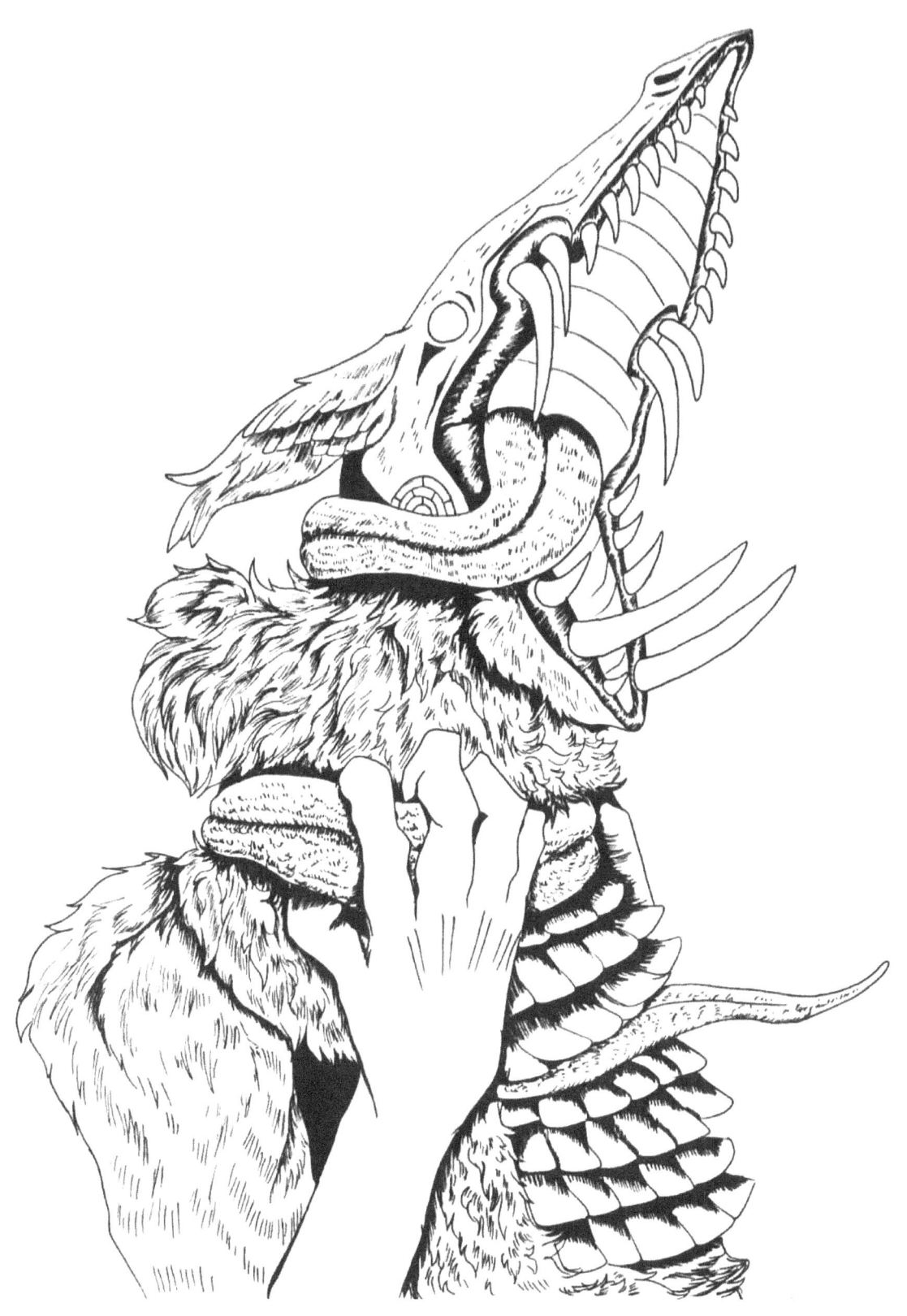

In the castle east of the sun and west of the moon

keeps the prince you so desperately seek.

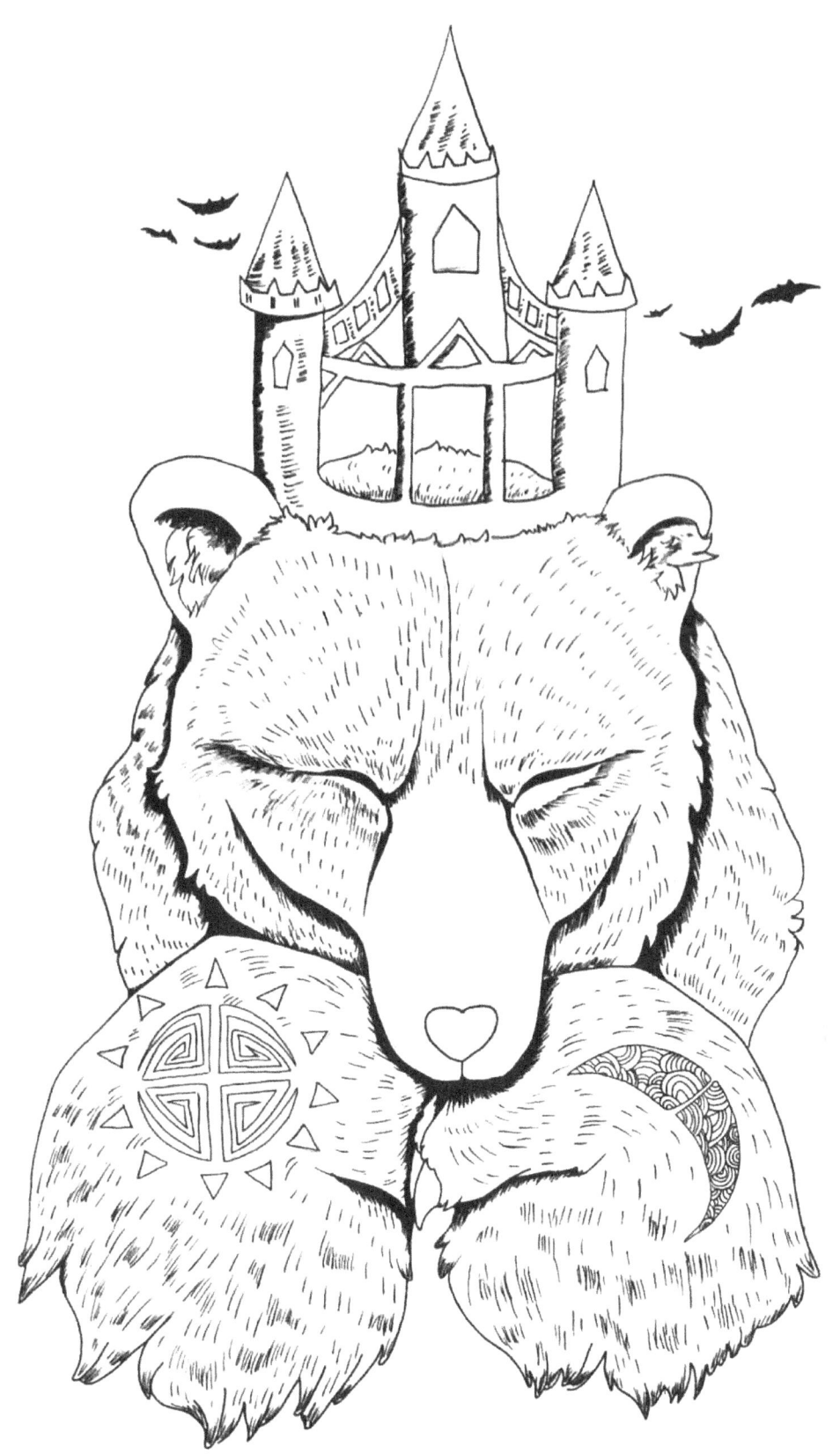

Jana's Creatures

What shall it be?

Step into the den of lies and you shall find the truth.

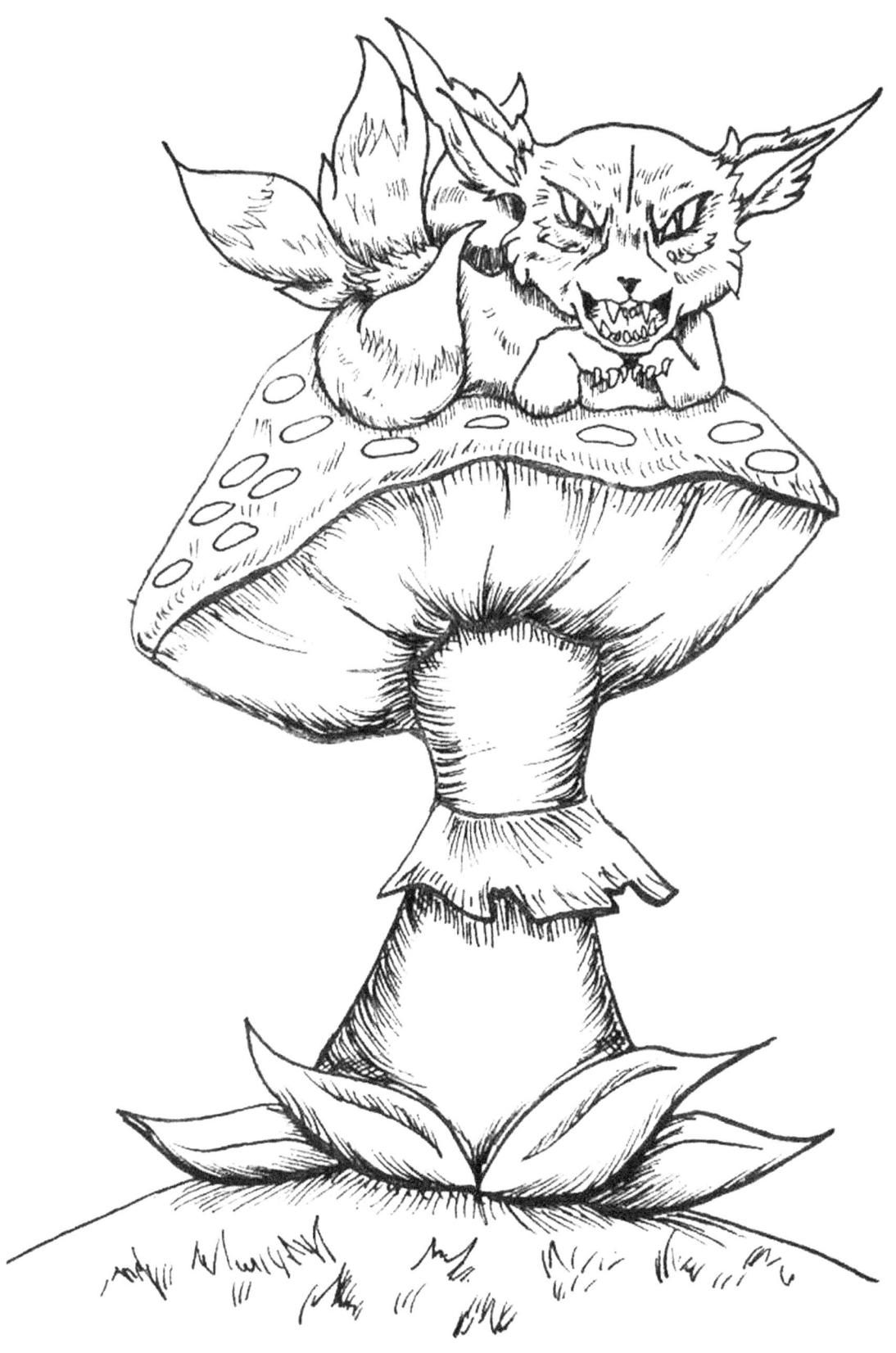

The lotus's white petals mask the sins

of humankind.

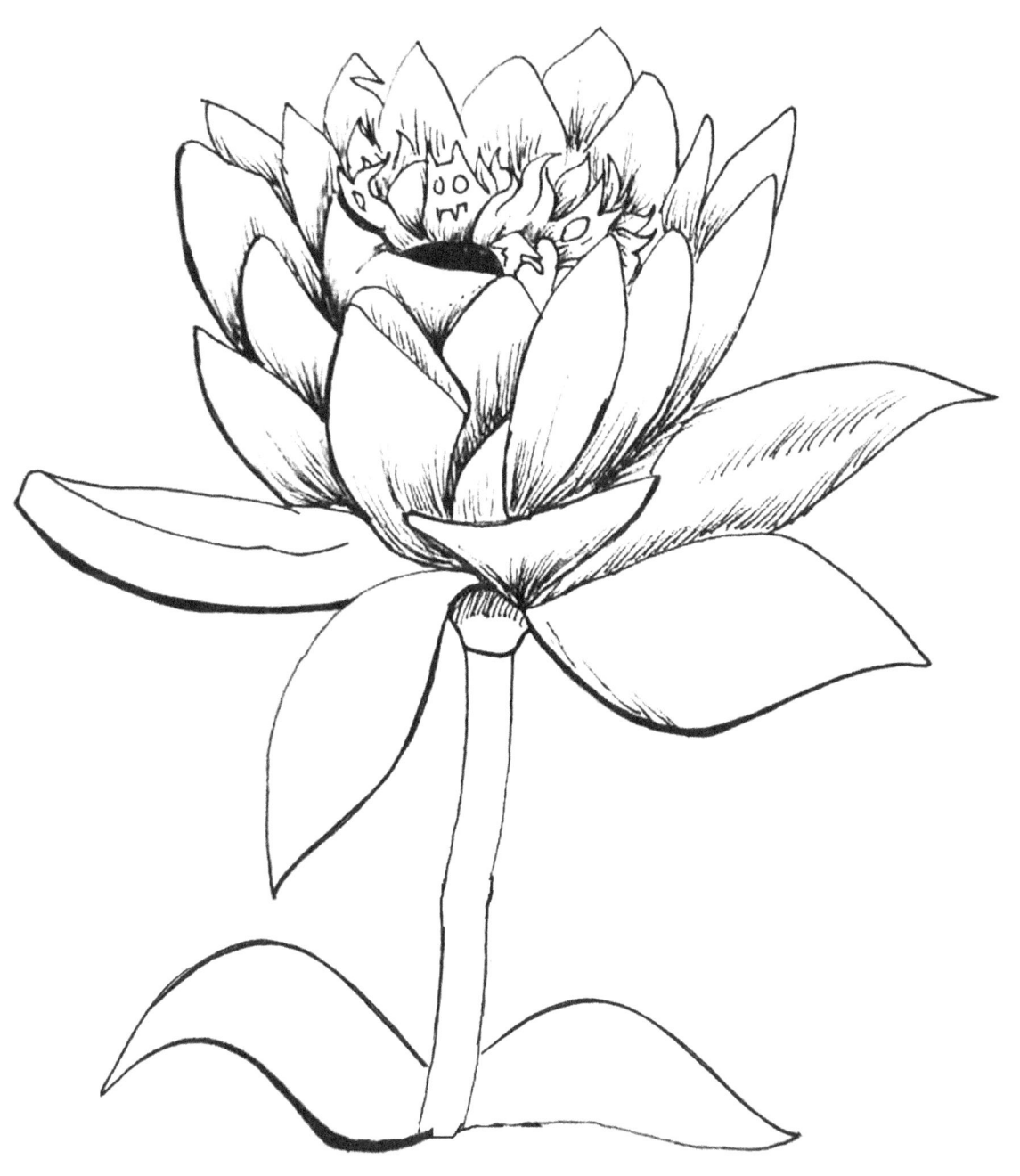

Her face was lovelier than the stars

shining bright in the sky.

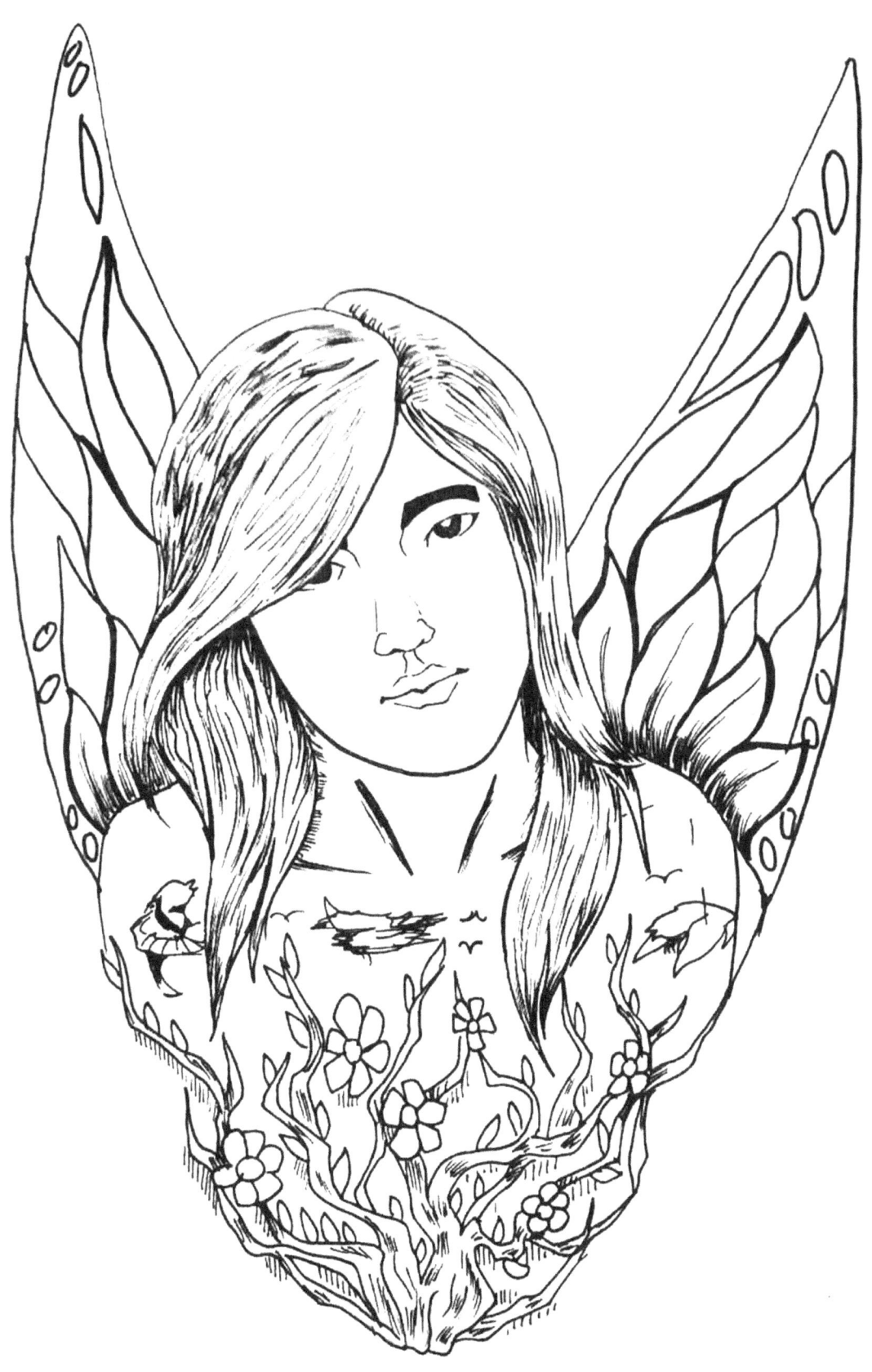

On the rocks lay the men lulled to their doom

by the mermaid's haunting song.

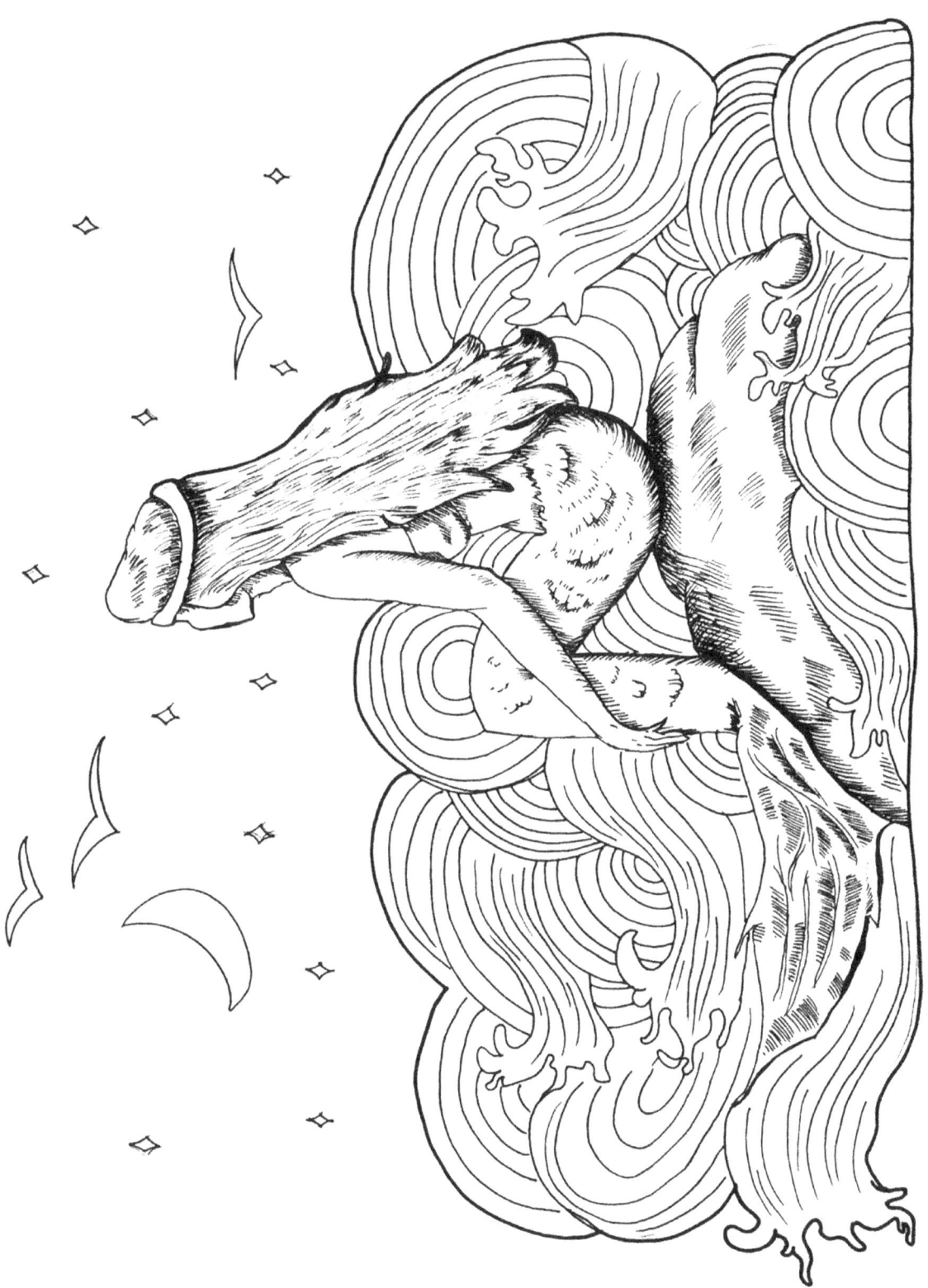

It is said that if a unicorn reveals itself to mankind,

there is truly no evil.

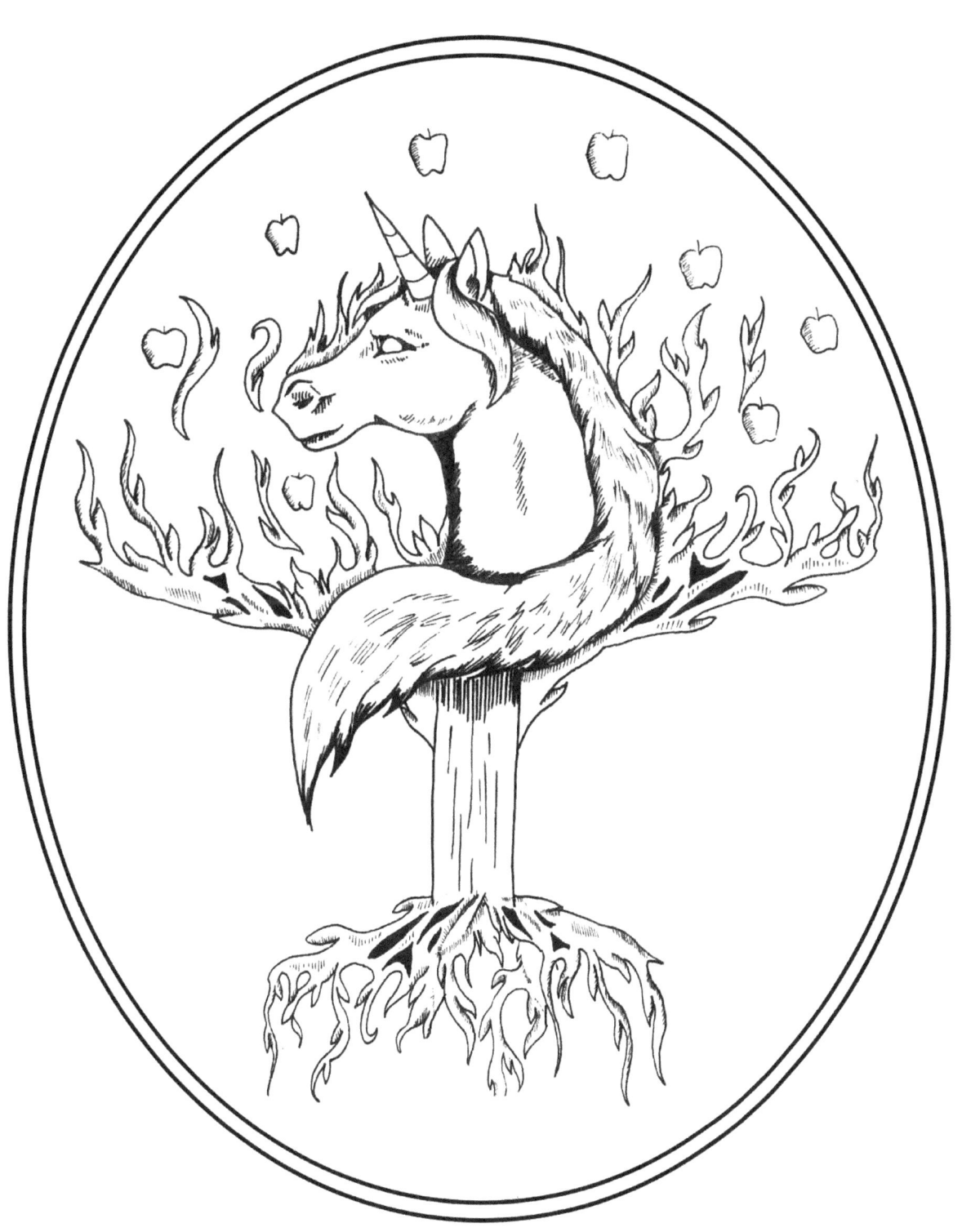

ABOUT THE ARTISTS

Adel Lee is a student artist from Singapore. Her family's frequent travelling allowed her to draw styles from different cultures around the world.

Jana al Faras is a student artist from Kuwait. Her works are inspired by many international art styles which continue to change in the developing future.

www.ingramcontent.com/pod-product-compliance
Lightning Source LLC
Chambersburg PA
CBHW081751170526
45167CB00009B/3998